FACING THE WORLD:

THE TEN PRINCIPLES

BRANDON HARRISON

Disclaimer

Published by H & W Publishing Group LLC

Dedication

This book is dedicated to the people who are constantly in the pursuit of staying positive and becoming the best versions of themselves.

Contents

INTRODUCTION

After graduating high school, I suddenly felt that it was time for me to make a change. I began to feel bored, and although I was just starting college and was employed, I found myself experiencing a sense of mental stagnation. As a result, I decided to read books on leadership, spirituality, self-improvement, and other related topics. With the help of these books, I began to feel differently about myself. I felt I had a reason to change my own narrative.

While I always understood the importance of education, I was never a fan of school. I felt that many of the subjects wouldn't apply to me in real life. I would have moments in class where I would sit and wonder how I could ever make practical use of the material I was being taught. How could the information I was being given really help me?

By deciding to look for books that interested me, I began to develop a greater awareness of the world. Reading provided me with new ways of thinking and expanded my mind in a multitude of ways.

My decision to start reading as a hobby became the foundation for how I would grow within my career and would come to understand life in general. By educating myself, I was able to appreciate more fully both the strengths I already had and my personal weaknesses.

This book will focus on the principles of success and the traits that many successful people have. Throughout this book, you will encounter examples taken from the lives of successful entrepreneurs from both the present and the past. A career in the corporate world has allowed me to accumulate a considerable amount of experience in dealing with diverse groups of people. I've had to handle terminations, counsel employees, and manage office politics on many levels.

A combination of workplace experiences and a rich personal life has allowed me to become a conscious observer and realize that a range of principles can be used not only to protect yourself but also to achieve your goals. During the many periods of change we are faced with, we constantly try to find ourselves and figure out the answers.

The challenge can be tough for an individual trying to balance daily life with the process of self-discovery. This will be a guide, written from the author's perspective, on how to face challenges in this world and succeed.

CHAPTER 1:

Be Your Own Competition

"I look in the mirror, my only opponent."
- Jay-Z

These days, people seem constantly stressed about becoming successful right away. The impact of social media has made it harder for people to stay focused on their goals without comparing themselves with others. Most people wake up in the morning and the first thing they do is check all their social media apps on their phones, such as Twitter, Instagram, and Snap-Chat. In doing this, a person is waking up to someone else's news rather than their own.

The constant information overload derived from social media can also cause a person to have a "group-think" mentality. This causes someone to deviate from their own viewpoints to agree with what's popular or trending.

It's important to avoid this because it will turn potential leaders into followers. If you study many leaders of the past, you will recognize a pattern. They were not intimidated into going against norms or ideologies that are present within society.

Don't get me wrong—social media can be a great tool for networking and even learning, but it can also be a distraction that should be limited.

There are certain habits you can develop that can help. On waking, don't check your phone right away; instead, allow yourself time to think and set goals for what you want to accomplish before you start your day. By doing this, you'll begin to use your time more wisely.

Your goals can be anything you want them to be, such as finishing an assignment for school, going to the gym, taking care of errands—anything that is productive to you. You always want to be better than you were yesterday. When focusing on your progress you will be focused on your own growth, not someone else's.

Social media has given people the opportunity to broadcast everything about themselves, but in most cases, you'll only read about people's accomplishments, not the low points in their life. Everyone has problems and the images being reflected on social media are not always what they seem. The sooner you decide to make changes in your life for the better, the more productive you'll be.

A way to continue along the path of being your own competition is to constantly focus on being a better person now than you were a week ago.

Bowing to pressure from your family and friends, you may feel compelled to follow a certain model of what people think is acceptable in the world. But if you aren't following the path destined for you, how will you ever be happy?

You should never limit yourself or place yourself in a box regarding what you can do before you've even tried. It's vital that you convince yourself you can do whatever you want to do. Be willing and open to trying anything that comes to mind.

One way to begin reprogramming your mind to think inwardly is to read over your goals before you go to bed each night or first thing in the morning. This will help to put you in the right frame of mind. Going to bed watching or reading content such as reality tv or gossip websites isn't the best way to end your night. Instead, you should try to feed your mind with positivity.

There's nothing wrong with enjoying reality tv or violent movies—I enjoy these myself—but it's best to be conscious of what your mind is consuming. Studies have shown that even music can have an impact on your mood. Pay attention to how you feel daily—your emotions can be influenced by the music you're consuming.

For the next thirty days, try changing what you are reading, watching, or listening to. If you think music doesn't have an impact on your current state of mind or your mood, you may be surprised.

Look back on the moments in your life when you needed motivation for something. It could have been at the gym. It could have been when you needed to complete a task. Think of the songs on your go-to playlist that you would listen to. I mention this to give you an example of how the content you consume can have an impact on your mental state.

CHAPTER 2:

Always Have Confidence, Never Arrogance

*"I have to cheer for me before anyone else
can cheer for me."*
- Kanye West

Self-confidence is necessary for anyone hoping to become successful. Many people's achievements are limited because of their lack of confidence in themselves. As a person trying to achieve their full potential, you will need to have confidence in everything you do; this will help you prevail over those who don't.

The key is to recognize when you're being confident and when you're just being plain arrogant. Confidence develops when you believe in yourself, have certainty about who you are, and have accepted both your flaws and your strengths.

Arrogance, on the other hand, occurs when someone is simply trying to impress or attract attention; they might well have an "I'm better than you" persona but they're just trying to cover up their own insecurities. Confidence can easily be mistaken for arrogance, but the people who have either of the two traits will certainly carry themselves in a distinct way.

No one likes an arrogant person; if you are always acting like you can do no wrong, the people around you will begin to build resentment toward you, and they may even hope something bad happens to you, so you can learn a lesson the hard way. Being arrogant can even ruin your chances of receiving good advice in the future.

Usually, when giving advice to an arrogant person, that person will become defensive and will not want to be told that they are wrong. The people around you will sense your temperament and it will make it even harder for them to feel comfortable giving you advice or explaining to you why you might be wrong because they won't want to argue with you.

I remember an instance when I met an individual who was probably in their mid-30s; I had to be around 19 years old at the time. During our conversation, the man began giving me advice on a particular subject, and I cut him off and finished his sentence for him. He paused for a minute, looked at me, and stopped talking. That's when I said, "No, you can finish", but he was offended.

At that moment, my need to show that I knew something resulted in me missing out on some potentially valuable information. From that lesson alone, I learned that even if I may know something already, sometimes it's best to be quiet and let a person finish their sentence.

There are times we may be embarrassed about not knowing something. Remember, though, that you are constantly trying to improve, and if you don't know something, don't be afraid to admit it.

This can be especially important in conversations you have with people older than you.

There will be moments where someone older may see somebody younger and want to educate them on something, but if they feel that individual may already have the answers, they may ask themselves what the point is, before moving on to advise someone who doesn't have the answers instead. Overall, this can be detrimental to you because you could be the one receiving that information.

Admitting Mistakes

Never be afraid to admit when you're wrong. There is a certain amount of freedom in doing this—people often respect others who can live their truth and admit to the mistakes they have made. This will allow you to earn the trust of others and it shows a degree of integrity.

The people around you will respect you for acknowledging your mistakes, and this will help you grow as a person because you will become more open to accepting wisdom along the way.

You must be able to find the same joy in losing as you do in winning; losing should not be seen as a failure but simply as a learning experience. The more losses you experience, the more wisdom you will gain, and you should always be willing to see the beauty in losing.

If you're able to direct any anger or pain you feel from a loss in a positive direction instead of letting it become something negative, this will amount to a remarkable achievement in your life.

CHAPTER 3

Practice Delayed Gratification

> *"Before success comes to most people, they are sure to meet with much temporary defeat, and perhaps some failure. When faced with defeat the easiest and most logical thing to do is to quit. That is exactly what the majority of people do. More than 500 of the most successful people America has ever known told the author their greatest success came just one step beyond the point at which defeat had overtaken them."*
> *- Napoleon Hill*

There will be stages in life where you will need to practice delayed gratification. Delayed gratification simply means you need to set aside material items or anything that could take away from your financial resources or supply a distraction to your mental focus. We are faced with plenty of distractions throughout our daily lives, which can become dull and repetitive.

The daily grind of getting tasks done can be tiring and hard at times. But in our quest to reach our full potential, it's imperative that you practice delayed gratification. This will allow you to develop your inner strength and will show you how you can exercise self-discipline over extended periods.

Delayed gratification can be something as simple as not buying that new purse or those new Jordans because you have a bigger goal in mind. Instead of buying those Jordans, you may want to save that money to buy some property in the future. Some goals can take months or even years to accomplish, but they're often achievable if you practice delayed gratification.

The longer you can maintain your self-discipline, the larger your reward will be. All of this will bring you the satisfaction and confidence in yourself needed to create larger goals for the future.

"Looking at the fall collection in the Neiman's selection. I should cop this leather jacket and go buy another necklace but I gotta goal, gotta reach a level I ain't hit."
- Payroll Giovanni

Assets vs Liabilities

A popular podcast called "Earn your Leisure" states the importance of having assets over liabilities. Assets can generate money over time, whereas liabilities usually drain our resources. Liabilities don't necessarily have to be material items. They might also include activities such as going out to the club every weekend or eating out at restaurants every day.

In contrast, assets could include things like an air fryer, a cookbook, a lawnmower, or a course on how to cut your own hair. All these could be viewed as assets—that cookbook, for example, could teach you how to make food that you could sell, which would help you to save money, instead of you going out and buying food.

The biggest asset you have, though, is your mind. Things like books, courses, seminars, and consultations can help you to develop a healthy mindset. If your mind is in good health, everything else will begin to fall into place.

You may be familiar with the term "the game is in me not on me" which can simply mean that although financial resources may come and go, the knowledge that a person accumulates could never be taken away. For example, you'll see millionaires who have lost their entire fortune be able to recover after a financial setback. In contrast an individual who has lucked up and won the lottery usually will go broke within 7 years according to *ABC news*.

Millionaires don't depend on luck but will rely on the information they have learned to regain their wealth. The lottery winner in most cases will not return to the financial level they were once at because they never learned how to earn a substantial amount of money or save for that matter. Therefore, it's imperative to have "the game in you and not on you."

The late, great TV show host Larry King represents this example perfectly. Throughout the 1960s, Larry began to gain his experience within the media industry as a radio interviewer for WMBM radio. While employed for the show, he indulged in bad spending by excessively gambling and other vices. Due to Larry's bad habits, his personal debt reached well above $350,000 forcing him to file for bankruptcy in that same year.

During this time, King is hired by WIOD Radio station to host a late night talk show. After years of working at WIOD, he gets on CNN'S radar, and by 1985, Larry is hired to host, the now famed, "Larry King Live" show. Larry died in 2021 with an estimated net worth of $50 million, after hosting his own television show for over 20 seasons.

Larry's story signifies that if someone possesses a level of knowledge or skill, they will always be able to accumulate a level of wealth.

> "Your strongest muscle and worst enemy is your mind. Train it well."
> - Anonymous

Another way to cut out unnecessary spending is to get rid of the vices in your life, such as impulse shopping, smoking marijuana, drinking, or gambling. All these things can be considered vices.

"If you find you have dug yourself into a hole...
stop digging."
– Robert Kiyosaki, from Rich Dad Poor Dad

The key to achieving delayed gratification is exercising patience. Without patience, you will never be able to sacrifice time or money in your efforts to reach your goals. Having patience allows you to think ahead and plan accordingly.

A Plan

When you are trying to achieve your goals, it's always best to have a plan written out. This will provide you with an instruction manual for carrying out the tasks you have in mind. Without planning, the chances of you achieving your goals will be limited.

For example, if someone is looking to save a certain amount of money, they should draw up a plan. Here's a step-by-step guide to writing a plan:

1. Think of your personal talents and some activities that you're interested in.

2. Ask yourself how you can make money from your talents. Are you good at cleaning cars, for example? Are you good at cutting hair? Are you a good salesperson? Thinking about your talents and the things you are interested in can help you decide on a path to follow.

3. How many cars or how much clothing do you need to sell to get to that amount you want to save?

4. Now that you've drawn up a number and made the calculations, you can start to plan your activities.

5. Next, write down the number of hours needed to reach your specific goal.

Here's a breakdown example of how someone with a $30,000 salary can save $10,000. If you make $30,000 a year you will need to save at least 20% in year 1, which will be equivalent to $6,000. In year 2 if you save just 15%, this will equal $4,500. In two years, you have already saved over $10,000.

Now imagine if you decided to work extra hours, pick up a second job, or engage in side-hustles. You will have $10,000 even faster.

Write down a plan and stick with it and see how fast your money can grow. If you find that you aren't able to save this amount of money due to other expenses, you can still use this as a blueprint for calculating what it'll take to save a certain amount of money, even if it takes longer than the two years mentioned earlier.

Just by writing down a simple plan, you have created new energy in the air. You're effectively creating an opportunity for yourself. You are taking direct action over how your future will be.

Now that you have seen the steps required to achieve that $10,000, you should continue to follow these steps for all of your other goals. Having set plans will keep you aligned with your goals and your long-term development.

"It is unfortunate there's some people judge others by their choice in foods, beverages, suits, watches, motor vehicles, and such; to them, superior people have excellent taste and in consumer goods, but it is easier to purchase products that denote superiority than to be actually superior in economic achievement. Allocating time and money in the pursuit of looking superior often has a predictable outcome: inferior economic achievement."
– Thomas J Stanley

CHAPTER 4:

Embrace Change

We are constantly facing change throughout our daily lives. Change often comes at random moments in our life when we aren't expecting it. The changes that tend to affect people the most usually occur in relationships, school, or work.

Changes that occur within our relationships are often foreshadowed by our parents. Most parents warn their children that the relationships they build with people during high school will not last once they graduate.

Most young adults are excited when they graduate from school and begin a new stage in their lives, but they are often anxious about not knowing what to expect in life after school. The key to overcoming this fear lies in anticipating what is to come. The changes that happen immediately after high school and college will prepare them for changes throughout the rest of their life.

Anticipating change can be hugely beneficial, and you must welcome change because it will help you to become resilient while also giving you the skills to adapt to whatever life throws at you. The best way to prepare for change is to be proactive and view change as positive rather than negative.

Self-Reliance

Many students fear life after school because of their dependence to friends and family. During school most students are living with roommates in dorms or apartment buildings while others may still be at home with their parents.

Parents may feel that they are protecting their children, but if students' needs are consistently provided rather than earned, they can stunt their growth into adulthood. When children don't possess the freedom to make decisions without the input of their parents. This can also affect their decision-making skills. This can lead to them depending on the approval of others.

According to *Berkeley Political Review,* "overprotection can lead to higher risk of psychological disorder, strong coping systems, and chronic anxiety." Take a look at the following excerpt taken from the Berkeley Political Review website.

> *"A child that is not allowed to take risks or make his or her own choices is bound to face a lot of anxiety and trouble when having to face the harsh realities of a chaotic world."*
> *– Ryan Chae (Berkeley Political Review)*

Relying on your parents for all decision-making and financial support can cause you further pain once it's time to live a life without school. To proactively gain independence needed after graduation, enforce a self-reliant mentality.

Oftentimes when someone knows they have a safety net at home, they choose not to go as hard as they should. If someone knows that their parents will be able to save them during financial setbacks, they will become lazy.

Hustler's Mentality

If you look at most go-getters, they usually have a strong work ethic. You see the self-sufficiency in their energy and the way they carry themselves. They understand that in life you must have a hustler mentality. If you do have the privilege of having individuals or institutions that help financially, you must begin to rebel against that safety net.

Strive and grind as if you only have yourself to depend on. By doing this, you prepare yourself for independence in the future. You want to be proactive not reactive, so take the time, if you are still in school, to build that independent spirit.

If you choose to wait until graduation for independence, you will suffer because you never built the skills needed. Now you will be on your own within a tough and a changing workforce.

Remember that change pushes you in the direction of growth, without which you will either stagnate or go backward. People tend to go backward to remain in their comfort zone. It's much harder to move forward because it's uncomfortable. Challenge yourself. Staying in your comfort zone is equivalent to staying in a loser's zone.

Aim to create opportunities that will shape your future. Imagine yourself at your highest potential. Once you have that vision in your mind, behave as that person. Encompass the behaviors associated with achieving that level of success. By seeing yourself in this way, you are shaping your future.

Have faith in yourself.

"We are really good at remembering the past, but we need to remember the future"
- Joe Dispenza

If your goal is to be successful in life, it's important that you move forward mentally, physically, and spiritually. Constantly placing yourself in a position of growth will have a positive impact on you financially. I am not saying a person should become a risk-taker and live a "you only live once" lifestyle; I am saying no one should be afraid to change the narrative of their own life for the better.

> *"The secret of change is to focus all of your energy, not on fighting the old, but on building the new."*
> *- Socrates*

Change can begin with small steps; for example, if you go to work the same way every day, decide to start going a different route. That could break up some of the routine steps you take each day.

You can implement changes in an uncomplicated way, such as trying different foods or even watching new movies instead of continuing to watch "Paid in Full" every week. Go to places you have never been to in your city or surrounding cities. These are all ways of opening your mind. When you begin to open your mind, you cause yourself to think in a unique way, and this will help you to gain a different perspective.

CHAPTER 5

Face Your Fears

"Either your fear consumes you or you become a bit insensitive. And you start to approach the problem instead of run from it."
– 50 Cent

We are constantly in a battle with ourselves when facing fear. Fear is dangerous because it will hold you back. Many people have unfulfilled dreams and ambitions that were never followed because of fear.

Fear is not all about worrying that you are going to get hurt or robbed by a person. That is *paranoia,* which is completely different; a heightened sense of paranoia can be great when used for self-preservation, but fear in most cases will not help you. Fear is something that limits your purpose in daily life; you fear being ostracized by society, you want to blend in, and fear being judged.

In life, everyone has dreams of becoming something—for example, people often dream of becoming actors, entertainers, athletes, or simply wealthy. But if you fear taking strategic risks or are not bold enough to stand out, you will never realize your dreams.

Experience Different Cities

The first step in becoming fearless is not to do something reckless but to try something bold. An exercise I have often used to overcome fear involves taking bold action. For example, I may randomly decide to go to a place I've never been to by myself.

While I am in this new city or state, I actively make the decision to speak to the locals and move around like I am from the city. I will go to bars, events that are going on in the city, and the local food spots. While doing this, I will be talking to locals and asking questions about the city I am currently visiting.

This causes me to be in a position where I am uncomfortable and forces me to adapt.

When I'm speaking to the locals, I always make an effort to engage with a wide range of different people. If I'm at the bar and an elderly couple is sitting next to me, I will speak to them. I don't discriminate regarding the people I speak with. You can learn from anyone, especially when you're an outsider in a new city, and speaking to different people allows me to gain a better understanding of what's going on in the world.

I was once in downtown Pittsburgh. It was my first time visiting the city, and as I was walking down the street by myself, I happened to see a middle-aged woman walking on the same sidewalk as me. I randomly asked the woman, "what's going on in the city tonight?" She smiled and said that she wasn't from the area but that she had "a group of crazy women on the way to her that should be here any minute".

Now, I started to wonder—a group of crazy women? What was she talking about? And sure, enough it couldn't have been more than 30 seconds before a party bus full of women in their mid-20s to early 30s arrived right there while the lady and I were conversing. Guess what? I was invited onto this bus. Mind you, I was alone.

This was a random trip—none of this was planned—but I spent the entire evening with these women, and it was a great experience overall. The women were complete strangers; some of them weren't even from Pittsburgh. Most of them were from different cities and different states as well. They were just there visiting, having fun with a friend that happened to live in Pittsburgh.

I left that night with a whole new understanding of life itself. Just by putting myself in a position to meet and be around different people, I was able to enjoy another great experience in life that showed me the benefits of being fearless.

You never know what kinds of experience you will have by putting yourself in the right position and speaking to people you may not usually spend time with. Once you start going to new towns and cities, you will gain confidence in dealing with a diverse group of people.

Fearing Success

Did you know that some people even fear success? Fear can affect your behavior in many ways, leading to problems such as procrastination, self-limiting beliefs, and a lack of self-discipline. Some of these actions can cause people to become self-sabotaging. You may begin to tell yourself that you can't travel, for example, or you can't open that business because it's too risky, or you have bad luck.

Instead, you should begin to ask yourself what you need to do to be able to take that trip or open that business. You should also ask yourself why you always have bad luck. Are your actions leading to negative outcomes?

By taking responsibility for your own thoughts, you will begin to formulate answers rather than simply making excuses that will continue to bind you to the mindset of a victim. Having a victim mentality will reinforce your negative thoughts and keep you in the comfort zone that is preventing you from reaching your highest potential.

> *"Your only limitation is the one which you set up in your own mind."*
> *- Napoleon Hill*

People can fear success unconsciously; they worry about what will happen to them when they begin to become successful. With success comes added pressure, and you may begin to feel the need to maintain a certain public likeness.

> *"Most people do not really want freedom, because freedom involves responsibility, and most people are frightened of responsibility."*
> *- Sigmund Freud*

We've all heard the saying "more money, more problems". Most people are subconsciously aware that with success can come negative energy. Don't worry about this.

You may begin to lose the support of certain family members or friends in your quest to become the best version of yourself, and this, though unfortunate, is part of life. You're not supposed to stay the same, remember—growing and evolving is what keeps a person going.

Always remember, too, that people hate up, never down. Continue to be positive and goal-oriented and you'll begin to see the type of opportunities and people you'll attract into your life.

CHAPTER 6:

Stay Mentally Sharp

"No drugs or alcohol, so I can get the signal clear as day, put my Glock away, I got a stronger weapon that never runs out of ammunition so I'm ready for war."
- Andre 3000 from the song "ATLiens"

To stay focused, you are going to have to strive to acquire as much knowledge as possible every day. Throughout our time at school, we read the material given to us by our instructors, material that may not actually apply to what we will experience in real life. The best thing we can do is to start educating ourselves.

Think about what your own interests are and look for material that will strengthen your knowledge. Don't wait on someone else to supply learning material for you. Once you have taken the initiative to begin your own self-education, you will gain a certain sense of freedom because you won't be relying on an instructor or institution to teach you things.

"One of the best things I did was to educate myself. I never really excelled in school after elementary and middle school. But I was always very intelligent, and I was smart enough to pick up a book, one that I was interested in and read about myself to try to learn myself. Once you know yourself you know what you want if you don't know yourself you don't know what you want and that's a problem."
- Nipsey Hussle

The best way to begin self-educating is to become interested in a wide range of different topics. By doing this you will start to identify reference points that can be used later in your life. The way you accumulate knowledge is to begin reading books on various subjects.

"Read absolutely everything you get your hands on because you'll never know where you'll get an idea from..."
- Malcolm X

As I mentioned earlier in the book, I personally enjoy speaking to a variety of different people. You never know what you might happen to learn from such conversations.

Using Time Productively

One time, I met with an experienced attorney for lunch. During our conversation, he told me that he reads a book a month. I was surprised because, aside from being busy with his day-to-day responsibilities as an attorney, he also has a family and actively participates in many community organizations. My awareness of how busy his schedule is made me realize how I can manage my time better.

Staying focused can be one of the hardest challenges. We are faced with many distractions that can make it difficult to maintain a high level of concentration.

There are times when we may be faced with boredom, which can cause us to look for time-fillers. One time-filler that can easily become problematic is addiction, whether it is to alcohol or other drugs. This can affect you not only financially but also mentally.

I'm not saying there is anything wrong with smoking or drinking but it's best to avoid overindulgence. We want to be as productive as possible, and having a clear mind is imperative when it comes to productivity.

Overindulgence in alcohol, drugs, or anything else for that matter, can be seen as a coping mechanism for dealing with stress and might provide a temporary escape. But we should try to replace those unhealthy habits with something that will help us in more positive ways.

How you spend your time will affect you in different ways. We all have moments when we waste time, but the key is to not make this a habit.

If you're finding it hard to stay motivated or focused, it may be due to your workload. I'm all for working hard and being productive but balance is also key, and there will be times when we are doing too much. Trying to grind on with this and that can consume a lot of energy and may not be sustainable.

Prioritize Alone Time for Yourself

A way to balance this is to allow time for yourself when you aren't doing anything. Cut your phone notifications off and go ghost for a day if you need to. When I talk about "going ghost" I'm simply suggesting you stop making yourself readily available unless it's for something that really cannot wait.

There is nothing wrong with just being in your own world for a moment. These days, we are easily accessible to others, which can lead to you not having the time to isolate yourself and get your thoughts in order.

When I talk about isolation, don't assume I mean being locked in the house all day. Go to the gym, walk a trail, take a road trip, anything that will help you to clear your mind.

By allowing yourself time to take a break, you will be able to come back to whatever task you're working on with a higher productivity rate. Remember to work smarter, not harder.

"Study the lives of the great people who have made an impact on the world, and you will find that in virtually every case, they spent a considerable amount of time alone thinking. Every significant religious leader in history spent time in solitude. Every political leader who had an impact on history practiced the discipline of solitude to think and plan. Great artists spend countless hours in their studios or with their instruments not just doing but exploring their ideas and experiences. Time alone allows people to sort through their experience, put it into perspective, and plan for the future."
- John C. Maxwell

One of the best ways to stay focused is to limit distractions in your life, such as unnecessary drama. Drama will cloud your mind because it can cause. Since drama creates useless energy, it's best to try to avoid it.

How productive do you think you can really be if you're always dealing with drama in your life? You want to limit stress as much as possible. We want our minds to be free. Being bogged down with unnecessary problems will cause us to become preoccupied with things that are not beneficial to us.

"Stop getting distracted by the things that have nothing to do with your goals."
- Sean Combs

Forgiveness

Something that can be stressful is holding a grudge. Many people have issues with forgiveness. If you're having a tough time forgiving someone, this will cause you to hold onto useless energy from your past. Charge it to the game. Keep it pushing.

By forgiving someone you are in effect releasing any power this person may have over you. Think of a person who may have insulted you—imagine if you decided not to take their insult to heart?

One way of bypassing this problem is to not take things personally. If you can manage this, you will keep yourself in good spirits. You should always aim to become better, never bitter. By holding onto negativity, you may be pushing new opportunities away.

Of course, we all have feelings, and I'm not saying don't stand up for yourself. But what I am saying is try your best to play past someone who may be trying to get a reaction out of you.

> "Even when a situation seems so personal, even if others insult you directly, it has nothing to do with you. What they say, what they do, and the opinions they give are according to the agreements they have in their own minds... Taking things personally makes you easy prey for these predators, the black magicians. They can hook you easily with one little opinion and feed you whatever poison they want, and because you take it personally, you eat it up..."
> - Don Miguel Ruiz

CHAPTER 7

Choose Your Friends and Associates Wisely

> *"If you look at the people in your circle and don't get inspired, then you don't have a circle. You have a cage."*
> *– Nipsey Hussle*

You should aim to keep the stress in your life to a minimum. One way of doing this is to choose the right people to have around you. Pay attention to your energy when you're around your friends.

If you notice that a certain person or group of people brings out your negative qualities, such as gossiping or being negative in any way, it may be best to remove yourself from those people or surroundings. Gossiping is never something you want to engage in. The people who gossip to you will be the same people gossiping to someone else about your business.

When the gossiping begins, try to pivot the conversation into something else more positive. If you gossip, you will risk saying something you can't take back, and this can be damaging to your reputation. Refrain from gossip.

Being Around the Right Energy

A good sign that you're around the right group of people is if you notice you are being challenged or taught something. When I say challenged, I don't mean insulted or judged. At first, this may be uncomfortable, but you may encounter different ideologies that force you to view aspects from an unfamiliar perspective.

Even if you aren't necessarily learning from someone, just being around a person who is trying to grow is beneficial. It's common knowledge that the people we choose to be around daily will affect us in different ways.

In the article from Harvard Business Review, "Primal Leadership: The Hidden Driver of Great Performance," written by Daniel Goleman, Richard Boyatiz and Annie McKee studied the impact of "mood contagion" within the workplace. Throughout this study they focused on how the mood of leaders impacts the success of their companies. It was found that leaders who had a more optimistic outlook and positive approach were able to inspire their employees, creativity would increase, and the level of critical thinking rose.

In contrast, when a leader was found to be negative it caused a lack of creativity, fighting between employees, and a decrease in profits. If you are around negative people daily, it will impact you subconsciously. You may feel like your energy is draining, your motivation decreases, and you may slip into a negative cycle.

Learn from Successful Peers

For example, during Jay-Z's rise to fame, he was taken under the wing of an older rapper who was famous in his neighborhood. This rapper's name was Jaz-O, and at the time he was more experienced than Jay-Z and had gained greater exposure.

During their time together they would rap and compete against each other to better their craft in the art of rap. By taking the time to learn from a wiser individual, Jay-Z was able to develop skills that would benefit him for the rest of his career.

> *"I connected with an older kid who had a reputation as the best rapper in Marcy—Jaz was his name—and we started practicing our rhymes into a heavy-ass tape recorder with a makeshift mic attached."*
> *- Jay-Z*

Jay could've easily chosen a different route when meeting Jaz. He could've decided to not be under Jaz's tutelage and allow for Jaz's level of success to create insecurity and uncertainty within himself. This would've been taking the easy route.

Often times, people can feel superior when they are the smartest person in the room but once another person who is on the same or has a higher level of intelligence, social status, or financial resources comes around their insecurities will begin to appear. This is a sign of a person who isn't truly confident within themselves because an individual who is sure of their own talents can appreciate when someone else of stature is in their company.

Let's take Dwayne Wade for example. In 2010, both he and Lebron James played for the Miami Heat basketball team. Although this team had been usually led by Dwayne Wade, once LeBron joined, he was the leader.

Wade allowing such a shift in roles only magnifies his humility. In the end, this change resulted in the Miami Heat team winning, not one, but two championships. Dwyane could've easily tried to sabotage this team knowing the blame would've fallen on Lebron, but his confidence allowed him to be the best teammate possible.

We can at times feel threatened by people who we perceive as more knowledgeable or wiser—a critical flaw. In certain instances, it can cause us to become envious of the other person, leading us to say to ourselves, "this person is a know-it-all," or "he or she is just lucky," which can turn into a subconscious form of hate. Instead, try to learn from a person even if you don't agree with all their ideologies.

If you notice any of the envious traits mentioned in someone in your life, or within yourself, you'll need to rectify this immediately. You can begin the process of improving this within yourself by allocating that energy towards something productive. Focus on how you can better yourself rather than hate on the next person.

"Surround yourself with hustlers because hard work understands hard work."
- Biggs Burke (Co-Founder of Roc-A-Fella Records)

Start mirroring the habits of those who are successful and see how far this can take you in life. Think about how you can develop those habits and ideologies that work best for you. I'm not saying you should agree with anything and everything someone says but you should look for things that you think might be beneficial.

Even as you are reading these chapters, you may find yourself agreeing or disagreeing with certain points, but if you're able to take something away from the book then that's a positive. Another strategy is to spend time around people older than yourself.

Mentorship's

While wisdom comes with age and experience, not everyone who is older than you is necessarily wise. However, if you're able to find older mentors who will share with you the knowledge they have accumulated over the years, this will be beneficial to your growth.

If you were wondering who you should take advice from, look at a person's achievements in their life. Are they living the kind of life that you would like to live one day? This can be a great indicator of whether you should take their advice or not. You can learn from both the success and failures of a person which will help dictate your decision making process.

We often see the results of success in the form of status symbols. A person may have a nice car or home and a good career or profitable business. But what we need to focus on is how they obtained these results. What traits does this person possess? How do they think? What do they do each day that has allowed them to reach this level of success? People usually see the shine but never the grind that's needed to achieve success.

Understand that learning from older generations can save you a great deal of time and could prevent you from making mistakes. There is a saying out there that claims, "a smart person learns from their own mistakes, but a wise person learns from the mistakes of others." That's why it's crucial to speak to people who are older than you—they have been there and done that. You should always be willing to listen to advice that could change your life for the better.

"I like to talk to the old schoolers, O.G. players, 'cause they was my age—I ain't never been theirs. I count on them for guidance, leadership, and advice. 'Cause everything I'm going through they done been through twice."
- Earl Stevens (E-40)

CHAPTER 8:

Maintain Humility

"There is always someone doing better than you and someone doing worse."
- Anonymous

At times, it's best to show humility. It's important to have the confidence to believe in yourself but being humble will take you a long way too. Humility should not be mistaken for timidity.

You simply need to focus on developing small gestures that you can use when you are communicating with others. A simple "yes, sir" or "no, ma'am" can create a long-lasting impression when you first meet someone, especially if you are discussing business.

Being timid can create a sense of awkwardness, which is an impression you don't want to give. Always try to carry yourself with an air of confidence. This will encourage people to trust your judgment and they will be more comfortable following your leadership.

Humbleness is a trait you will need to develop, especially when you start to attain some level of success. When a person becomes flossy or excessive in trying to convince others that they are successful, this can come across as bragging. There is nothing wrong with doing well in life, but bragging is something to be avoided.

Being less conspicuous about the way you live or the projects you're working on can generate a certain degree of security around you. I'm not suggesting you become a recluse and never speak to anyone. On the contrary, you should network, shake hands, and continue to live an active social life. Just be conscious of what you share. Your success will either motivate others or make them jealous of you.

Look at Floyd Mayweather Jr, an athlete from Grand Rapids, Michigan, who earned over 1 billion dollars from his career, retired undefeated, became a successful businessperson, and is now one of the most hated athletes in the world. There may be other reasons why he is hated but it's clear that much of that hate is caused by him flaunting his wealth and bragging about his success.

"I don't fight for legacy... I don't fight for none of that. I fight for that check... I'm in the check-cashing business."
- Floyd Mayweather Jr.

Personally, I'm motivated whenever I see an elevated level of success. It shows me that anything is possible if you continue to work hard in everything you do. But you must realize that not everyone views public success in the same way.

Did you know that, in the past, certain kings would give back to their citizens things such as food and other items to avoid the repercussions of being wealthy?

Some kings of the past knew that if they didn't share their wealth with their community, they could become the target of potential violence from an envious population. One king known for giving back was the King of Mali, Mansa Musa, who is thought to be the richest man who ever lived, with a net worth that would total $400 billion today. Mansa Musa earned his wealth from trading salt and gold.

In 1324, Mansa went on a pilgrimage to Mecca that lasted up to two years. During his journey, he carried over 300 pounds of gold with him. Mansa would end up giving away so much gold to the citizens while traveling through Egypt that the value of gold would decrease over the following 12 years, according to *National Geographic*. Mansa understood the importance of being humble and giving back. He also understood the importance of empowering others.

We can all learn from Mansa Musa's approach to humbleness. A way you can begin implementing this approach in your own life is to become more involved in your local communities, through which you can spread joy and share wealth.

Even if you don't have the financial resources to give back, you can dedicate time and intellectual property to organizations that support positive causes.

By doing this you benefit both others and yourself. People will view you as a person of value because you truly are.

> "If you walk through life and don't help anybody, you haven't had much of a life."
> - Fred Hampton

CHAPTER 9:

Become a Great Observer

Listen more than you speak. I'm sure we've all heard that quote before. It sounds so simple. But this is harder than you may think because it requires discipline. Most people love talking about themselves. If you know how to use this to quote to your advantage it will benefit you greatly.

I recall a time when I was interviewing for a higher-level position. During this interview, I decided to say as little as possible, and instead focused on asking the interviewers questions. Now, I know what you're thinking. Wait, you were being interviewed?

But you decided to ask the interviewers questions? What do you mean by this? Well, let me explain.

During the interview, I was careful with the words I used. Of course, I mentioned my work history and my hobbies, but right after that, I shifted my attention to the interviewer. I began asking them questions such as

- "What would it take to be a good fit at this company?".

- "How has this company been affected by COVID?".

- "What's the culture of this company?".

- "What's the retention rate?".

While asking these questions, I used a pen and a notepad to write down their answers for them to see. Now, by asking direct questions, I was able to turn the tables. By the end of the interview, it was as if they were selling themselves to me rather than the other way around. I left the interview confident, knowing I had secured the job.

Focus on Non-Verbal Cues

Listening doesn't just mean paying attention to words; it also involves seeing the nonverbal cues that may be present in social interactions. No matter how hard we try to control the events in our lives, there will always be setbacks. In a time of potential crisis, we need to be prepared.

People are often rendered powerless because they are caught off guard when something goes wrong. The key is to always be prepared. A way of doing this is to become more observant of your surroundings.

Let's say you're at a job and, suddenly, the energy appears to be off. Managers are spending less time around you, speaking to you less, or even giving you looks that make you uncomfortable. You should be aware of things like this.

Pay attention to what training you're not receiving. If you notice another employee is receiving more training than you, you should take note of this.

Training signifies that the company you're working for is investing in you and is planning to employ you for an extended period. Pay attention to everything. Once you see such behavior, this will confirm to you that it's probably time to make a move.

People will never say to you that they're about to replace you, but their actions will. If you're able to read between the lines and interpret the body language of others, you will be one step ahead of everyone.

Use Your Job to Create Your Dreams

It is also crucial to learn as much as possible while working at any company you're employed by. Take the necessary steps to gain as much information as you can and use this information for your own benefit. Try to learn how the company is run.

- How do they hire employees?

- How's their training program?

- How do they create budgets for the overall success of the company?

Begin asking these entry-level questions to gain a better understanding of the organization of your employer. By doing this, you're preparing yourself for establishing your own business. Learn as much as you can.

Here's an example of how an employee can use his or her paid time for their own benefit. Let's say you work at an accounting firm. You've been learning the process of how to prepare budgets, compute taxes, and run audits. By learning the general accounting process, you will be able to use your skills to form your own tax business or accounting firm in the future.

Look at Sean Combs (P-Diddy), who started his career as an intern for Uptown Records in New York. Sean always had a love of music, and this passion made him an avid club-goer. While he was living in New York he saw many music videos of upcoming talent shot around the city.

Combs would see the music moguls working behind the scenes, who would usually have the large cell phones, jewelry, and power, which were all the things he aspired to have for himself. He would take note of which record labels his favorite artists were signed to, record companies such as Def Jam and Uptown Records. Although Sean didn't have any experience working in the music industry, he decided to call these companies daily and offer to work for free.

The records companies didn't know what an internship was, but Sean did because he'd heard about internships from the medical students at Howard University, the college he was attending. Combs was able to explain the concept of an internship to Uptown Records' founder Andre Harrel, who was thrilled at the thought of someone working for him for free. This was all the opportunity Sean needed.

Sean, who was already going to school at Howard, had to take a 4-hour train ride just to get to Uptown Records. While working as an intern, he was able to prove himself and worked his way up to an A&R position after two years of working for free. He was eventually fired as an A&R manager but two weeks later he created the music label that is known today as Bad Boy Records.

Although he was fired, he used his time at Uptown wisely, learning as much as possible about the industry. His internship provided him with the knowledge that would allow him to explore future opportunities. This success wasn't down to luck; instead, it was a result of Sean taking full advantage of his opportunity and learning as much as he could while in his position.

> *"I would sneak on the train and work two days in New York and the rest of the days I would spend in Washington DC in college, and it was a hard time, but I was pursuing my dream and I didn't really have any money to eat and no money to get back and forth. But I would stay focused because I knew I was going to make it one day."*
> *- Sean Combs*

There are countless other examples of successful people who used their internships as planning opportunities that would benefit them for the rest of their lives, such as Spike Lee, who started his career as an intern at Columbia Pictures before he began directing his own films. Movies directed by Lee have now grossed over $585,306,732 in worldwide box office sales according to *The Numbers* website.

Always think of an exit plan. If you're comfortable with being an employee, that's fine but let's start to think bigger.

Observe Social Interactions

Another useful tactic is to observe the ways a person treats other people. In interactions with people, you will notice if a person is warm or cold toward you. The way to decide this is simple.

Have you ever seen how someone is with a friend? Usually, they are warm; they may greet the friend with an open embrace, a hug, a strong handshake, or a smile that causes their eyes to light up. All of these are indicative of a person being happy to see someone.

Now, pay the same attention to how they treat you. They may shake your hand with less enthusiasm, have a cold smile, or barely speak to you. This may be a sign that this person is not your friend or that they genuinely dislike you.

One thing to observe is the person's eyes as you engage with them. Some people just focus on a person's smile. But look deeper into this. I want you to pay closer attention.

Next time you meet someone and they appear to smile, look at the individual's eyes. Are they wide and lit up or are they tight and forced? The latter could be a sign that they are not genuinely happy to see you. This may seem trivial to you, but I promise you it is a reliable means of figuring out how a person truly feels about you without them saying a word.

> *"While our faces can be very honest and explain how we feel, they do not always necessarily represent our true sentiments. This is because we can, to a degree, control our facial expressions and, thus, put on a false front. From an early age, we are taught by our parents not to make faces when we don't like the food in front of us, or we are compelled to fake a smile when greeting someone we don't like. In essence, we are taught to lie with our faces and so we become quite adept at hiding our true sentiments facially, even though they occasionally do leak out"*
> *- Joe Navarro*

Now that you know potential signs to look out for in another person's body language, think about how you present yourself when you are speaking with others. How's your posture? Are you making eye contact with the individual while they are speaking to you? Is your body facing them during your conversation?

All these signs will show the person that you are talking to that you're listening and present in the conversation. Listening will increase your level of emotional intelligence while also leaving a positive impression on the people you interact with.

CHAPTER 10:

Keep an Open Mind

The key to having an open mind is to be non-judgmental. Even if your aim is to help someone, this can be taken in the wrong way and people's feelings can be hurt. Sometimes it's best to just listen. Critical comments can lead to resentment.

Meet people where they are in their life. Don't try to change a person or force your views on them, and remember we all have our own journeys to make. The people who are open to receiving this information will make themselves apparent. Even if you begin learning new things you still won't know everything.

Now, there are times when a person may come to you for advice and ask for an honest opinion. If you're in this situation and do have to give advice, avoid saying things such as "How did you make that mistake?", "I could've told you that", or "You should've known better".

When you say things like that, you're going to make a person feel worse than before. Be calmer, more relaxed, and show empathy. You can, instead, say things like "We all make mistakes", "Thank you for coming to me about this", or "Let's try to think of the best way to solve this".

By doing this, you're showing that you are willing to work with the individual to figure out the best solution to the problem at hand. Even after all of this, though, I would still recommend refraining from giving advice unless you really must.

Remember that none of us are perfect. We are all trying to grow and become the best versions of ourselves that we can be. In the process of doing this, we will have made mistakes—plenty of them—and will continue to do so. It's part of life. Some people call these experiences "growing pains"; I simply call them living.

Whenever you feel inclined to criticize someone else, ask yourself, "Have I made this same mistake before? Do I really know this person enough to cast judgment?" Probably not. You may have heard a rumor about this person, but you have never heard their side of the story. Focus on your own flaws before you begin to judge someone else's.

Keeping an open mind also applies to situations where you're conversing with someone you may not like. For instance, you may be in a room with a person who has different political views but who also just happens to be a successful businessperson. Now, are you going to agree with this person's political views? Probably not. But are there things they can teach you about the business sector? Possibly. The only way to find out is to have a conversation with that individual.

Never close yourself off from information. Having a closed mind prevents you from gaining knowledge. Remember, you should think long-term; by doing this, you will be basing your decisions on logic rather than emotion. There will be times when you will receive criticism from others. In these moments, allow yourself to hear the person if the criticism is constructive.

Being open to criticism will allow people to make you aware of the flaws in your character that you may not be able to see. This will help you tremendously because you will then be able to address those flaws.

Final Thoughts

I'm appreciative of you for taking the time to read this book. The understanding I've gained from life has shown me that we are all trying to grow into the best possible versions of ourselves. Don't focus on perfectionism; focus on maintaining a level of integrity based on the principles and character you already have, and trust that everything will fall into place. I hope this book has been of value and has given you a perspective that you may have not had before. Don't keep this book a secret. Pass it along to others and if you would like to reach the author, you can contact me at youngdreamerclothing@gmail.com

Much love.

About The Author

Brandon is the founder of Young Dreamer Clothing, which was established in 2018, and also works as a human resources professional. As of right now, he lives near the Detroit, Michigan area.

www.ingramcontent.com/pod-product-compliance
Lightning Source LLC
Chambersburg PA
CBHW060349130626
46553CB00003B/1156